I have
CEREBRAL
PALSY

I have CEREBRAL PALSY

**Brenda Pettenuzzo
meets
Maria Hill**

Photography: Chris Fairclough

Consultant: The Spastics Society

01029

FRANKLIN WATTS
London/New York/Sydney/Toronto

Maria Hill is eight years old. She was born with cerebral palsy. She has a younger sister, Angela, aged five, and a younger brother, Keith, aged two. Maria and Angela both go to the Barking Church of England Primary School. Keith stays at home with their mum, Georgina. Their dad, Paul, is a printer. The family lives in East London.

Contents

© 1988 Franklin Watts
12a Golden Square
LONDON W1

ISBN: 0 86313 699 0

Series Consultant: Beverley Mathias
Editor: Jenny Wood
Design: Edward Kinsey

Typesetting: Keyspools Ltd

Printed in Great Britain

The Publishers, Photographer and author would like to thank Maria Hill and her family for their great help and co-operation in the preparation of this book.

Thanks are also due to the Barking Church of England School and to The Spastics Society.

Brenda Pettenuzzo is a Science and Religious Education Teacher at St Angela's Ursuline Convent School, a Comprehensive School in the London Borough of Newham.

The early years

"At first my mum and dad didn't know that I had cerebral palsy."

"Cerebral" means brain, and "palsy" means damaged. Having cerebral palsy means that the part of the brain which controls movement does not work properly. This can be caused by something which happens before a baby is born, during birth, or in the first years after birth. In Maria's case, doctors believe that the damage was caused while she was being born. At some stage her brain did not get the oxygen it needs to work properly, and it suffered some damage.

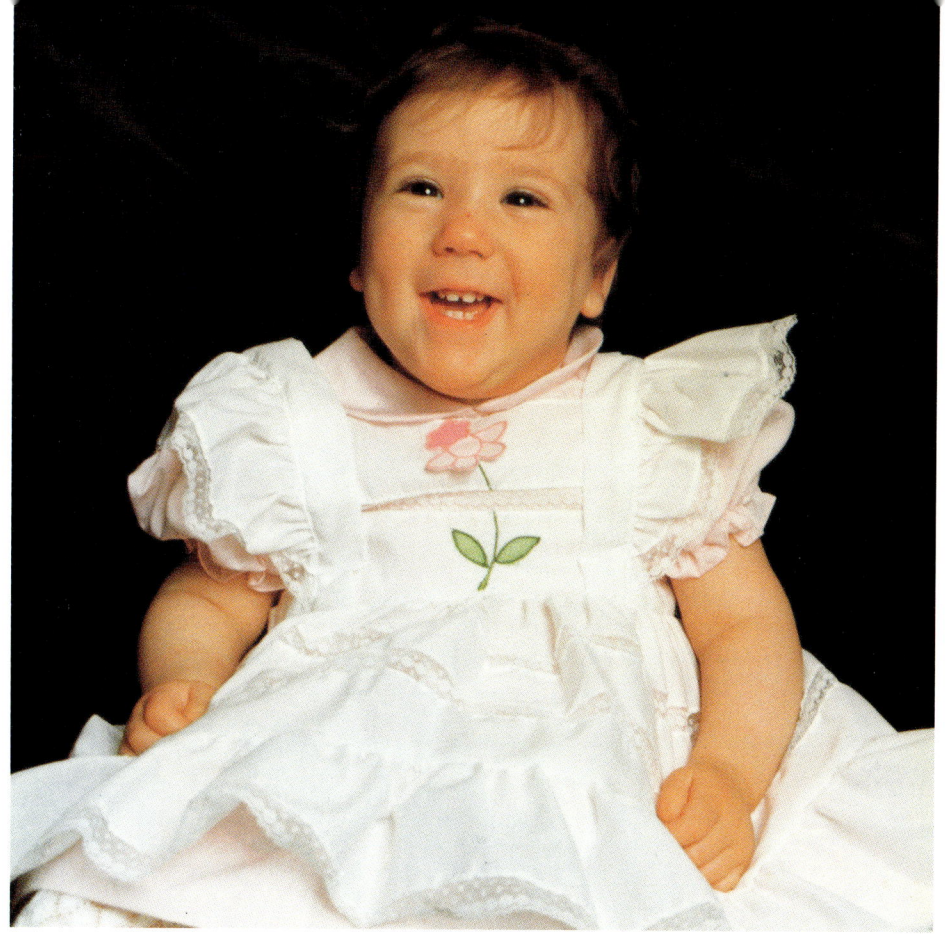

"I was about eight months old when the doctor told my parents that I had cerebral palsy."

Maria was a happy baby. In most ways, she made progress just like other babies. But her parents noticed that her legs were often straight and her feet crossed. This was not what other babies' legs seemed to be doing. At a routine check at the Child Health Clinic the doctor decided to refer Maria to a hospital. The specialist doctor there told her parents that she had cerebral palsy. Soon afterwards, they contacted The Spastics Society. A social worker came to visit them. Since that time they have found The Spastics Society a great source of support in every way.

Life today

**"I usually manage to get about the house easily.
Sometimes I need a little help."**

When Maria was smaller she had hardly any use of
her legs. She could only crawl, as many babies do, on
her tummy. Help from various physiotherapists and
her mum have made it easier for her to stand. Now
she can get around by leaning on the furniture, or
holding on to someone bigger.

"I like to play in the garden. We have a sloping path so it's easy for me to get in and out."

Maria is like most other children of her age. She likes to play outside, even if it is raining. Her mum or dad usually puts a piece of carpet on the path. Maria can get up and down the path on her own, but if they did not put the carpet down she would soon wear out the knees of her trousers and tights (or her knees themselves!).

"Our house has a lift on the stairs, so that I can go up and down on my own."

When Maria was small her parents used to carry her up and down stairs, just like any other child. As she grew older and heavier, carrying her became more impractical. She can climb the stairs, but this is difficult and tiring. It might also be dangerous if she were to fall. The lift was installed a few years ago. Many people with physical disabilities have similar lifts fitted in their homes.

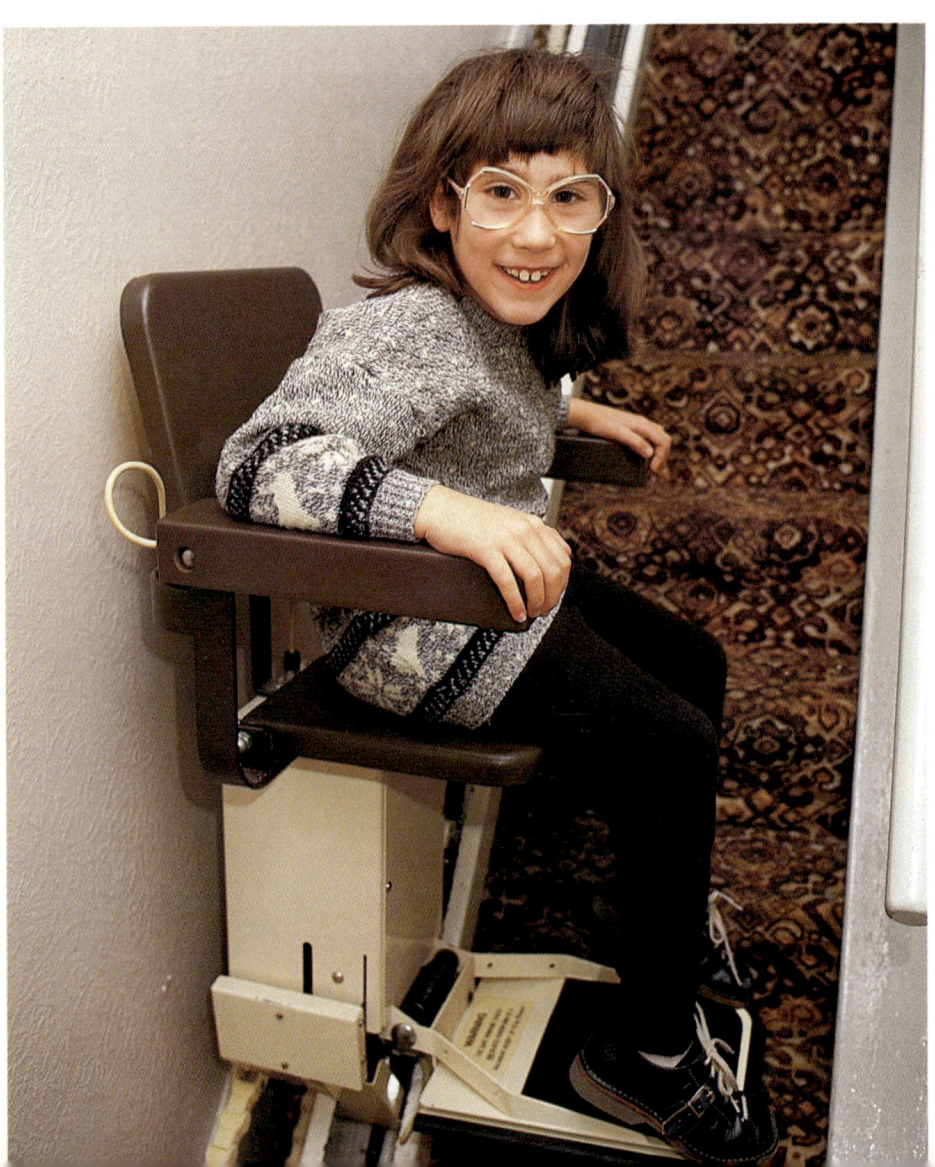

"I have my own occupational therapist. She gives me homework which helps me with the things I find hard to do."

Cerebral palsy has affected Maria in ways which are not all visible. She has difficulty with some types of thinking as well as moving. She finds it very hard to judge the way in which things fit together in space. An occupational therapist is trained to help people with all sorts of practical problems. Maria's occupational therapist gives her games and other things to do which help her with these problems.

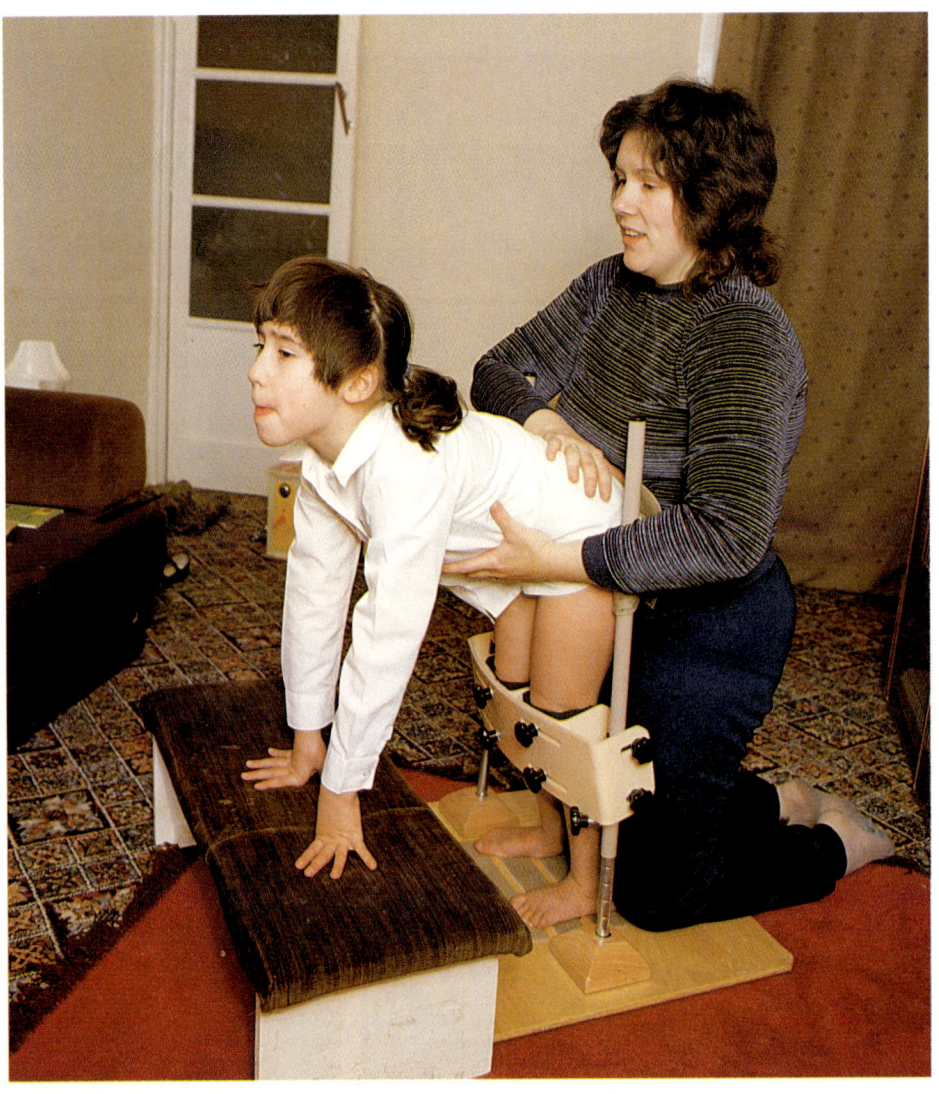

"I have to do lots of physiotherapy. My mum makes me do it every day after school."

A physiotherapist comes to see Maria at school every three weeks or so. Maria also visits a special centre for children with cerebral palsy in the school holidays. Her mother has learned exactly which types of exercise are helpful to Maria and helps her to practise at home.

"Sometimes my sister helps with my 'physio'. I do some of the exercises on a bench and some in my standing frame."

Maria has found that she can move more easily because of the physiotherapy. She doesn't always enjoy doing it, though. Her mother tries to make a game out of the exercises. It helps if Maria's sister can join in. Angela enjoys herself, and Maria has more fun.

"Every day I have to put on my special boots. My mum usually helps me get ready for school."

Maria has special boots which support her feet. When she is standing, it is very important that her feet are supported. The boots help to keep her feet on the ground in a more normal position than she can usually manage. She has two or three pairs of boots. She can change from one pair to another before they get uncomfortable.

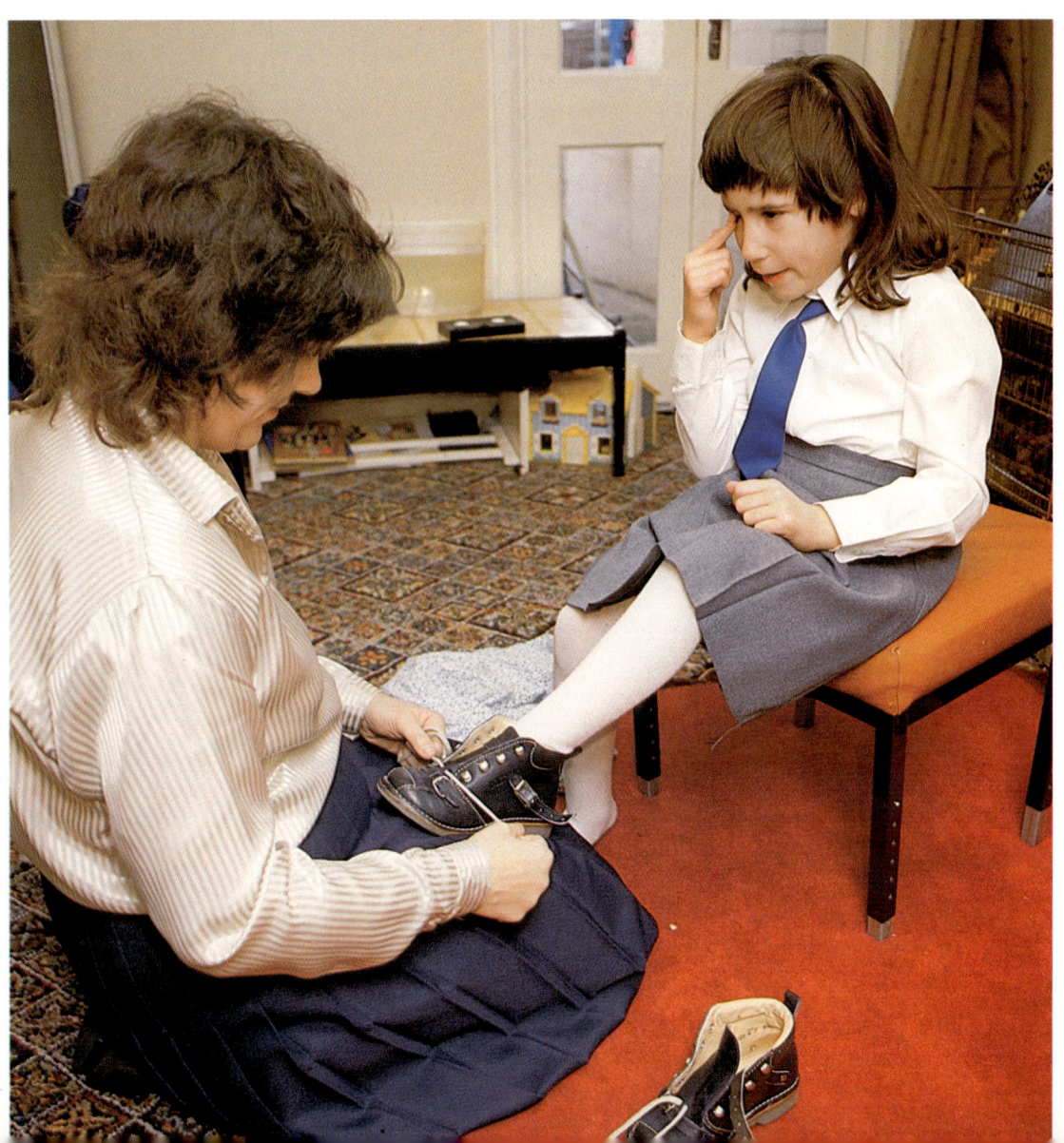

Disabled Person
Please Leave
This Space Clear.

"My mum takes Angela and me to school, but Keith has to come too. We go in the car."

If Maria's mum couldn't take her to school, she would probably have to go in a taxi. It would be much too difficult for her to get there on the bus. There is a ramp at the front of the house to make it easier for Maria to get out. Her mum and dad try to make sure that their car is always right outside the house. They have a special sign on the garden wall asking other people not to park in front of the house.

At school

"My class teacher is called Mr Owen, but I have a special helper called Mrs Hanlon as well."

Mrs Hanlon is Maria's Welfare Assistant. She is on hand to help Maria during the school day. Maria does nearly everything that the rest of her class do. Sometimes she might take a little longer than the others to do things. Her reading is very good, but she finds it difficult to keep her writing neat. This is a problem shared by many people who have cerebral palsy.

"If the rest of the class are copying from the blackboard, Mrs Hanlon writes the work out and stands it on my desk."

Maria used to find it difficult to copy from the board. Her mother found a recipe stand which has proved very useful. Mrs Hanlon can make a copy of the work which the rest of the class are doing. The copy stands up on Maria's desk. Maria can see what she is doing, and work just as fast as the rest of the class.

"Some of my class go with me for special maths lessons with Mrs Lee."

Because she has cerebral palsy, Maria has a specific learning difficulty with maths. Mrs Lee is a special maths teacher. She finds out what each child's problem is then tries to help them overcome that problem. Mrs Lee has heard from Maria's occupational therapist. Together they are helping Maria with her difficulty in judging the way in which things fit together in space.

"I have a computer at school. Mr Spain and Mrs Hanlon are helping me to use it."

Maria is fortunate because her school, with the aid of a charity, was able to get a computer for her. The computer can speak, and a light-pen can be used with it. Maria can pick out words and assemble sentences using the light-pen. The computer will say the words to her, and when she has finished making a sentence, the computer can print it for her. Many people who are disabled find computers very useful.

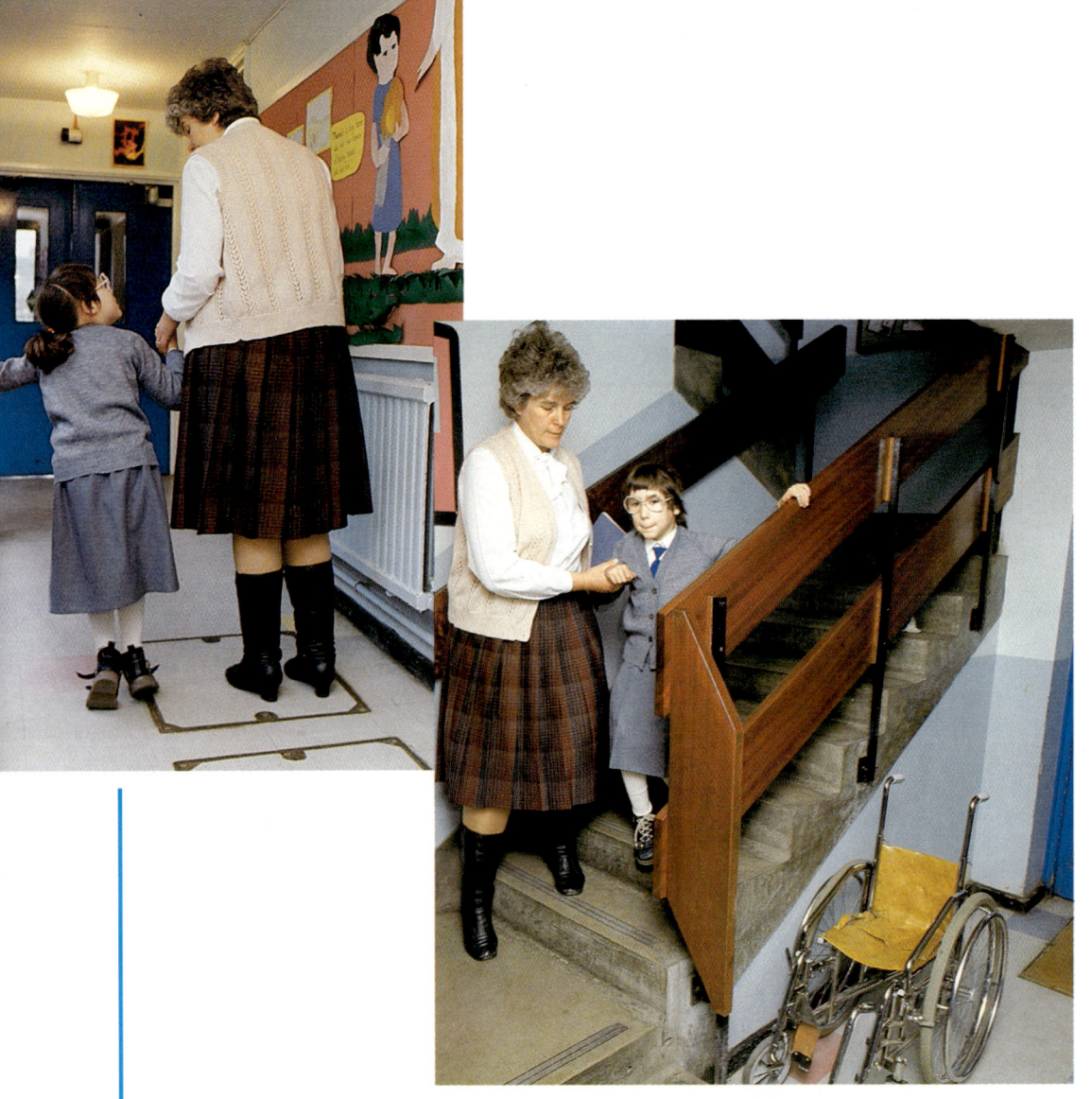

"If my class are doing games, I can't always join in.
Mrs Hanlon and I then usually go for a walk round
the school."

There is a wheelchair at school which Maria can use
but often she and Mrs Hanlon go for a walk round the
school. They look at the work of other classes which
is exhibited on the walls. Sometimes Mrs Hanlon does
Maria's "physio" at this time.

"I have another lady who helps look after me at dinner time. Her name is Mrs Flicker."

Mrs Flicker is a lunchtime helper at Maria's school. Most schools have helpers to look after the pupils during the lunch break. After Maria has finished her school lunch, she goes outside into the playground. Mrs Flicker stays with her. Maria often takes herself for a "spin" in her wheelchair. Sometimes she gives someone else a ride!

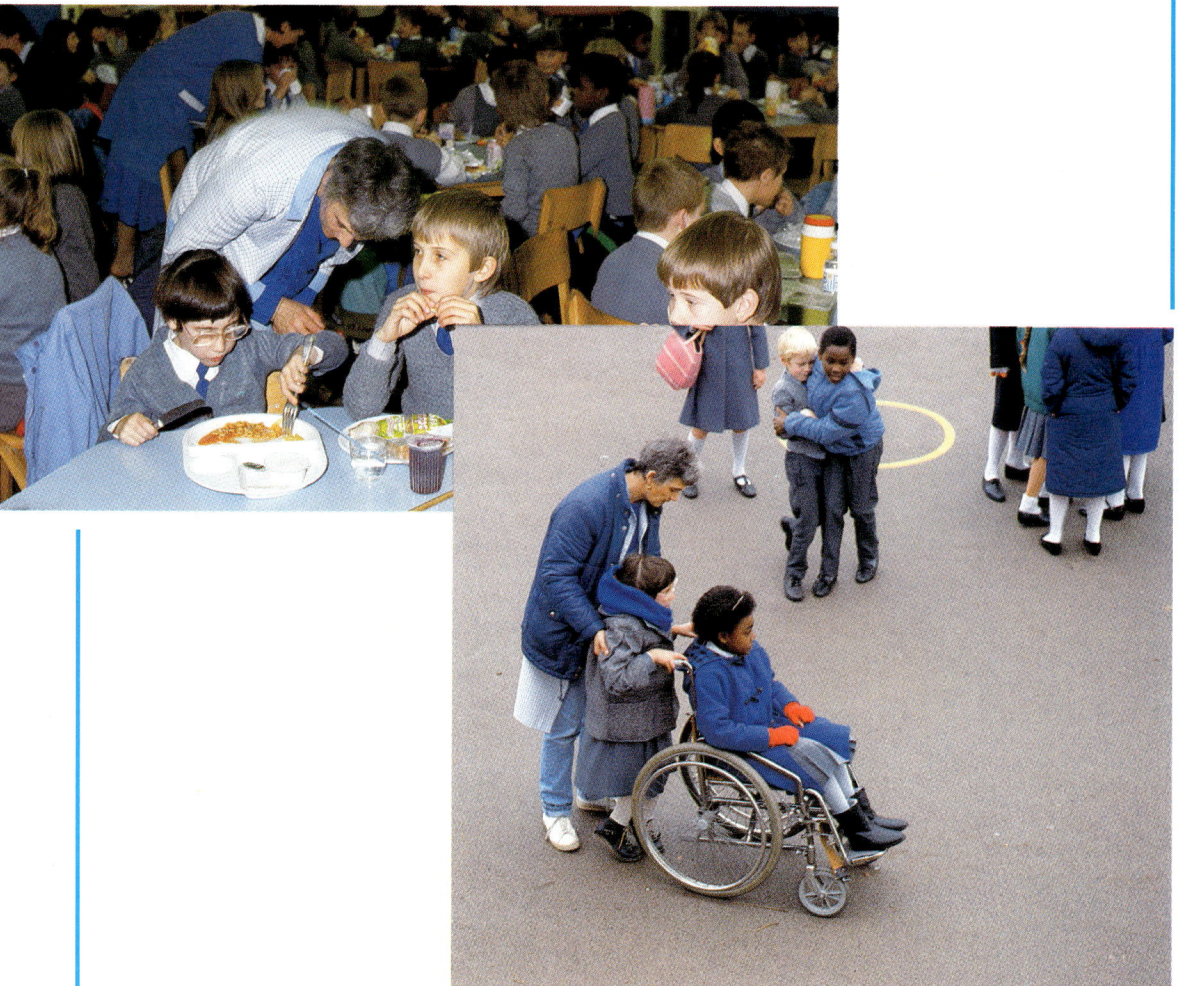

At home

"I've been a Brownie for nearly a year. I like going to meetings every week."

Maria is the only Brownie in her group who has cerebral palsy, but that doesn't make any difference to the way she enjoys herself. She has been able to join in all the Brownie games and activities. She is working to get her collectors badge. She spends a lot of time sorting out and adding to her collection of postcards.

"I belong to another club. It's called the Tuesday Club and it meets at my church."

Maria and her family are members of the Church of England. They go regularly to a church near their home. Maria goes to a young people's club at her church every Tuesday. It is another opportunity for her to play with other children of her age. Sometimes she sits in her wheelchair, and sometimes she manages without it.

"I have a frame which helps me stand. I use it for
'physio', but I can do lots of other things in it!"

There are lots of frames which children can use to
help them do various activities. Maria's frame holds
her in a standing position. It is good for straightening
her legs and for her posture. She has found that she
can do all sorts of things about the house like this.
She also enjoys getting wet as she cleans the car!

"A few years ago I couldn't do anything at all with my legs. Now I can almost walk."

Maria has recently been able to walk with the aid of her sticks. This is something which her parents had always hoped she would be able to do. She moves quite slowly, but she is getting better all the time. This type of exercise, and the "physio" which she does at home, will help to make her more mobile as she gets older.

"We all love the park. My mum and dad take us there as often as they can."

There are several parks near to Maria's home. With three children it isn't always easy to get out. Maria's family go out together whenever they can. Her younger brother and sister like to play in the playground. Maria likes this, and she enjoys feeding the ducks. Maria and her brother and sister are just like any three children in any ordinary family.

Facts about cerebral palsy

Cerebral palsy is not a single disorder. It is a term which describes a variety of conditions. These conditions can be caused by anything which damages the part of the brain which controls movement and so impairs its function. No two children are affected in exactly the same way, and various mixtures of problems are found. There is great variation in the severity of the disability caused by Cerebral Palsy.

The causes of Cerebral Palsy are classified into three groups based on the time at which the damage probably occurred.

Cerebral palsy may be caused before birth, as a result of some problem during pregnancy. General health problems, smoking, too much alcohol and the taking of certain medicines are all things which put many unborn babies at risk, but there is no evidence to suggest that any of these can cause cerebral palsy by themselves. Many of the reasons for brain damage occurring are not very well understood and so it is difficult to say exactly what has been the cause. Sometimes a mother may suffer from an infection while pregnant, but may not have had any symptoms herself. Three infections are known to cause brain damage in unborn babies: rubella (German measles), Cytomegalovirus, and Toxoplasmosis.

Birth problems can also cause brain damage – for example, severe haemorrhage from the womb, sudden separation of the placenta from the womb, or when the umbilical cord, through which the baby receives its oxygen supply, slips down the birth canal and becomes trapped. Each of these problems can cause a baby to suffer an oxygen shortage which results in brain damage. There are other complications of very premature birth which can also lead to cerebral palsy – for example, breathing difficulties, brain haemorrhage and severe jaundice. It is sometimes very difficult to diagnose cerebral palsy in a premature infant. If a baby has had a difficult birth it will need to be observed over a period of weeks or months. Cerebral palsy is often not detected in the first five months of life, until the child begins to develop co-ordinated movement.

Cerebral palsy may occur later in life as a result of certain conditions such as meningitis and other brain infections, and also severe head injuries.

There are three main types of cerebral palsy. The type of cerebral palsy a person has depends upon which parts of their brain have been affected most seriously by the original brain damage.

The cortex of the brain is the outer layer and is concerned with thought, movement and feeling. If this part of the brain is damaged, the most common form of cerebral palsy, called *spastic cerebral palsy* or *spasticity*, results. This means that the muscles are in a state of increased tension. Movement becomes more difficult and sometimes muscles and tendons develop a fixed tightness which is very difficult to relax. Spastic muscles do not always pull in the right direction, and it is not uncommon to find joints dislocated because stiff muscles have pulled them out of place. It is very important to start physiotherapy as soon as possible, so as to reduce the risk of complications because of the abnormality of the muscle tone in children who have this form of cerebral palsy. Not all children are affected to the same degree. When only half the body is affected (left or right) and the other half is normal, the child is said to be *hemiplegic*. Where the legs are affected but not the hands, they are said to be *diplegic*. When all four limbs are affected, the child is *quadriplegic*.

Below the cerebral cortex is a deeper layer called the basal ganglia. This area helps to organise movement. When it is damaged, the form of cerebral palsy which results is called *athetosis*, or *athetoid cerebral palsy*. The characteristic of this condition is jerky arm and leg movement. There are often unwanted movements which get worse when the child attempts deliberate movement. The state of muscle tone is constantly changing, and wriggling and writhing movements are often seen. Children with this type of cerebral palsy frequently have difficulty in communication because their tongue and vocal cords are affected. Hearing impairment is also more common in children who have *athetosis* than in other forms of cerebral palsy.

The cerebellum is the part of the brain which controls co-ordination and balance. When this is damaged *ataxic cerebral palsy*, or *ataxia*, occurs. This appears as clumsiness, poor balance, and jerky movements. An eye condition called nystagmus may also be present. When this occurs, the eyes show jerky movements when they look sideways. Speech is also rather jerky, and children are slow to develop speech.

Several other medical problems are sometimes associated with cerebral palsy. The most common one is intellectual impairment, or mental handicap. This can be mild, moderate or severe, but it always means that the child's development will be delayed throughout childhood. If a child has a problem in a particular area which is greater in magnitude than his or her other intellectual problems, then the problem is called a specific learning difficulty. Many children are apparently normal in every way but have one or two learning difficulties for which they need extra help in school.

When a child has severe or multiple disabilities their development is often delayed because of the inability to overcome their disability. Often a child's intellectual capacity or learning ability cannot be assessed because of the child's communication difficulties which need to be overcome. Microtechnology can be useful in helping such children to communicate.

There are other conditions which are found with cerebral palsy. The commonest eye defect is squint, or turning of one eye. This is usually treated with glasses or an operation. Another condition affecting vision is less easy to treat. Cortical vision defect is caused by a problem in the part of the brain which receives the messages sent to it by the eyes.

Children with cerebral palsy often have speech problems due to their lack of muscle control.

Some children have epileptic fits. It is not possible to predict which children will have fits and which will not. Some only have them when young and some develop them later.

The other medical problems which affect children who have Cerebral Palsy are minor. They may suffer from slow weight gain, constipation (due to poor muscle tone), chesty coughs and behaviour problems, which might be due in the greater part to the frustration they experience.

People who have cerebral palsy and their families can get a variety of equipment and aids from health services and local authorities. They can get advice from many agencies, both voluntary and statutory. There are several charities who are able to assist in the purchase of specialist equipment where the government or local authorities are unable to provide such things. More people than ever before who have been born with seriously disabling brain damage are being enabled to lead full and fulfilling lives. Improvements in facilities, advances in technology and the changes in public attitudes are helping to make this possible.

THE SPASTICS SOCIETY

The Spastics Society was founded in 1952 by a group of parents who were concerned about the neglected needs of their disabled children. Since then The Spastics Society has grown rapidly to become a large and diverse organisation which aims to serve the interests of children and adults with cerebral palsy providing support and advice for thousands of people.

The Spastics Society covers England and Wales, and along with its 187 affiliated local groups provides services in all aspects of education, care, accommodation, employment and welfare for people with cerebral palsy and their families. These services include schools for children of differing abilities, further education colleges, residential care, skills development centres, careers advice, playgroups, and respite care schemes. There is also a comprehensive network of social workers to provide support, information and counselling.

The Spastics Society has a small research budget whereby it supports projects researching into the prevention of cerebral palsy and ways in which its treatment can be improved. The Society is also a campaigning organisation which believes in the right of people with disabilities to lead as fulfilled and independent a life as possible as integrated members of society.

Further information and details of The Spastics Society's services and literature can be obtained from:

The Spastics Society
Publicity and Information
Department
12 Park Crescent
London W1N 4EQ
Tel: 01-636-5020

Please enclose a large, stamped addressed envelope wherever possible.

Glossary

Epilepsy A condition caused by bursts of electrical activity in the brain. It is not known why these occur, though it is thought that some people develop epilepsy because of brain damage caused by, for example, problems during birth or a road accident. Many people who have epilepsy have "fits", during which their muscles move jerkily and uncontrollably and they may become unconscious for a short time.

Haemorrhage Heavy and dangerous bleeding, caused by the bursting of a blood vessel.

Jaundice A yellow colouration of the skin which happens when the liver is damaged or infected with disease. It also occurs in many babies shortly after birth, and in most cases it disappears after a few days with no ill-effects.

Meningitis Inflammation of the membranes which surround and protect the brain. This can be caused by infection by a virus or one of various bacteria.

Muscle tone The proper firmness and tautness of the muscles. Muscles which are too floppy are said to be lacking in tone.

Occupational therapist A person who has been trained in using mental and physical activities to help people recover from or overcome the effects of disease or injury.

Physiotherapy This is the use of massage, exercises and sometimes heat treatment to treat people who are suffering from disease, injury or deformity. A person who is specially trained to do this is called a "physiotherapist".

Placenta An organ which develops inside the womb while a baby is growing inside its mother. The placenta passes food substances and oxygen on to the baby from its mother, and returns to the mother the waste products of the baby.

Umbilical cord The structure which joins a developing baby to its placenta. Inside the cord are the blood vessels through which the baby gets oxygen and food from its mother, and waste substances are returned to the mother. The cord is quite long so as to allow the baby to move around. After birth the cord is cut, leaving a scar called the navel on the surface of the baby's stomach.

Womb The organ in a woman's body where a baby develops before it is born.

Index

32